WRITING IS

A Poetry Anthology

Massillon Public Library Adult Writers Group

FORWARD

The Massillon Public Library Adult Writer's Group was established in February of 2023. It was only supposed to last the month of February, to help kick start writers' passion and to kick off the *Your Novel is Now* multi-month program at the library.

However, the writing group was such a success that it lasted far beyond February. Many of the writers have since released books, and grown far beyond any of them dreamed.

The group meets twice a month, and has supported authors with editing, formatting, proofreading, and, most importantly, encouragement.

In February 2024, the group decided to rebrand as the *Massillon Public Library Writers of the Round Table*.

Find all of the *Writers of the Round Table* collections on Queen Anne's Lace Publishing's website.

CONTENTS

WRITING IS

Existence Confirmation

Writing is the Who, What, When, Where,
and Why of Who I Am

What Saved My Life

An Escape

A Ballad and Dreams

Hard

Introspective

EXISTENCE CONFIRMATION

Alexxa Burton

Writing is...

     self expression

     self affirmation

     inner communication

     self confirmation

Writing is...

     being heard

     being known

     finding immortality

     being remembered

Writing is...

     forcing my voice into the world

forcing my words into the world

fighting my way up for air

forcing the world to accept my soul

Writing is...

a way to fly

a way to live

uncompromising freedom

a way to never die

Writing is...

not pretending

not compromising

being free with my thoughts and ideas

not hiding anymore

Writing is...

existence confirmation

WRITING IS THE WHO, WHAT, WHEN, WHERE, AND WHY'S OF MY LIFE

Lisa A. Beltz

Who I am and a bit of what I've always been. Who is both my adversity and friend that I seek to placate or attempt to please.

What I use to express my most trivial fancies and my deepest thoughts. What I use to entertain or to purge my soul of its pain or rejoice in its triumphs.

When I view the losses and gains of the past and look forward towards the future. Why I search my life wondering why I have been waiting and discovering the time to express myself in this way is now!

Where I soar to the heights of human existence in the mountains of my mind and plunge to the hellish-most parts of my being. Where I emerge cleansed and renewed.

Why I rise up early in the morn and work late into the night, looking with joy into the mirror before slumber, knowing the fulfillment of a good day's labor. Why I am able to be the person that I am.

WHAT SAVED MY LIFE

Dawn E. Dagger

Writing is

pen on paper

ink and dust

the force between

me

and myself.

Writing is

self-soothing -

like an infant

twisting their chubby fingers

in their mother's long locks of hair.

Writing is

the strength to burst

from the darkness

like a dandelion

in sidewalk cracks.

Writing is

what saved

my life.

AN ESCAPE

Crystal Hoff

Writing is

an escape for me

 to let my feelings

out on paper.

Writing

helps me forget

what's going on

in my personal life.

When I start writing

hours seem to fly by.

I love

to write

more

than anything else.

Writing

gives me a purpose

in my life.

I sit in my chair

and shut the world out

with its incessant noise.

All around me

is quiet.

My thoughts

drift to clouded skies

on the horizon.

Lands far away

and the green fields

of times past.

Then

I am ready

to write.

A BALLAD AND DREAMS

Donna J. Bunner

Writing is a ballad that has yet to be sung.

An expression of words that has not yet seen on a wall hung.

A simple text to say how you feel or an email to explain how things are for real.

A memo listing upcoming events and chores or a letter from a loved one you can save and adore.

A notebook of memories from all around or a spiral lined paper of handwriting collections that are wired and bound.

A scrapbook of ideas and thoughts or a short story of poems or plays whose lines are taught.

A list of dreams of one hoping to achieve or a group of words thought in your mind for one to believe.

A task that needs to be written down to be remembered or an illustration of pictures and words to be drawn in sand and sun.

HARD

MKS Cooper

Writing is…

Hard

Because writing words down

Means more than their sound,

Makes them lasting and real,

Makes you feel

What you try to hide and deny.

When you need words to last,

Not get lost in the past

You cry and you sigh,

But write the words anyway.

Otherwise, who can say

How it would have turned out?

Written words, no doubt,

Have clout, and staying power.

Spoken words can be heard

Then forgotten in an hour

Flown out of the mind

Like a startled bird.

Nevermore to be seen

Like written words

Or heard.

SELF-DISCOVERY

Dwight Parrish

writing is…

like standing

along the shoreline

examining the horizon

where the sky

touches the lake

of my soul

a boat

of emotions

drifting

without boundaries

without an anchor

without a sail

a basin

of thoughts

too vast

to comprehend

too deep

to surface

until waves

swash ashore

stimulating

my footing

leaving me

a message

in the sand.

WHO WE ARE

THE WRITER

MKS Cooper

I'm a person who's lost,

Busy living a life

Being a mother, a daughter, a wife.

Taking out garbage, mopping the floor

I sometimes don't know who I am anymore.

Then I sit at the keyboard and wait and wait,

And suddenly something opens the gate.

The words start to come, they spill, they pour,

The feeling of power makes my soul soar,

Now I know who I am, I'm not lost anymore.

WILDFLOWERS

Dawn E. Dagger

When I think

Of beauty

I think

Of a bouquet.

Perfect

Soft

Petals

And

Trimmed stems.

A dozen roses in a bunch

With no thorns.

I cannot be

A bouquet.

I have thorns

And tears.

But when I look

At the side of the road

And see

The wildflowers-

So hearty

And so

Wild

They are

No less beautiful.

In fact,

I am wildflowers

On the side of the road-

Wildly beautiful.

IN YOUR EYES

Dawn E. Dagger

They say

Beauty

Is in the

Eye

Of the beholder.

But most

Things

Are beautiful

To all.

Flowers

And sunsets

And shimmering stones.

These are all

Beautiful.

We can agree.

Unless,

Of course

Your aim

Is to be

Contrarian.

I have

Never

Felt

Beautiful.

A thousand things

I could pick

At myself

About.

A hundred things

I learned

As a child

Were wrong

With me.

My forehead

And my smile.

The way

I talked

And laughed

And existed.

Taking up

Too much space

Simply

By

Being alive.

But

When you turned around

And your breath

Hitched

And your

Eyes

Lit up

Like a thousand stars

 In the sky.

The way

Your jaw dropped

And every

Single

Fiber of your being

Relaxed.

The way

That all of your worries

Vanished In that moment.

The way

You whispered "you're beautiful"

In such

Soft tones

Like I was an apparition

That

Might vanish

Should you speak too loud.

In that moment

I knew I was beauty

In your eyes.

That moment

Changed me.

Fundamentally.

Forever.

I know now

That

I am beautiful.

THAT IS BETTER

Alexxa Burton

I am not like them

so I put on a mask and pretend

for their benefit

They are not like me

so I keep my mouth shut

and feel isolated

I am me

I like what I am in all my twistedness

I will not change

not for them

I stand tall

well short

and quiet in my isolation

so I don't offend others and protect myself

Hoping a like mind will present itself

sometimes I have hope

often that hope falters

most times that hope is proven wrong

I am the darkness that shines bright in the nothingness

I am the creation with a forte for creating

I am the passion born of sight and chaos

I am not like them

I am me

that is enough

That is better

DEMON'S IN THE DETAILS

Alexxa Burton

I see things in myself

I don't let others see

But there are hints

If you're observant

The demon's in the details

I hide it well

I've learned to play the part

Smile here, commiserate there

Pretend to be normal

The demon's in the details

The way my eyes go flat

When I can't share I don't agree

The way my tongue goes silent

When I know my thoughts aren't welcome

The way my anger burns

Burns hotter than those around me

The demon's in the details

The way I'm more comfortable in darkness

Than in the light of day

The way the fire enthralls my soul

But the earth fails to ground me

The way nature fails to sooth me

But the chaos of a crowd brings me calm

The demon's in the details

I am comfortable with who and what I am

I don't need the approval of others

I may not smile but I would not change myself

I am confident being me

The demon's in the details

Look at me with your eyes closed

When you can see me that way

If you can see me that way

Then you will see

The demon's in the details

STORM AND WIND AND RAIN

Alexxa Burton

I sing the song of the rain

It runs its tears down my body

Cold and merciless fury

I sing the song of the rain

A song of heat and belonging

A song of passion and longing

Like a lover's kiss you used to know

There's the wrath of the scorned

And the vengeance of all you've betrayed

I sing the song of the rain

I sing the song of the wind

Its call is filled with longing

Its heart is filled with pain

I sing the song of the wind

A song of deep seated dreaming

A song of hope ever fleeting

The torment of past serenity

The enduring ache of loss

And all the heart break you've ever known

I sing the song of the wind

I sing the song of the storm

Its anger as hot as fire

Its eyes as cold as ice

I sing the song of the storm

A song of restraint close to breaking

A song that's cold and calculating

Energy coiled about to spring

Ready for the attack

Ferocious violence and primal rage

I sing the song of the storm
38

Storm and wind and rain

KISS OF THE RAIN

Alexxa Burton

When I'm walking on dry land

I'm drowning in the air

When the rain falls down

The worlds crying my despair

And when the darkness falls

 I'm lost in its embrace and I am home

For it's the only home I've know

I see your face in the star light

I hear your voice on the wind

I'm not alone any longer

As the night closes in

I feel your touch on the wings of darkness

I taste your kiss in the rain

I know you stand here beside me

And I call out your name

As the moon rises

And as the sun falls

 The stars awake for the evening

And I answer their call

Why walk in the day light

When you can dance in the rain

Why drink in the brightness

When the stars call your name

Why play the games of the day

When all that you want

Is the nights embrace

The touch the darkness

The caress of the stars

And the kiss of the rain

NEARSIGHTED

Lisa A. Beltz

*"For now we see in a mirror dimly, but then face to face.
Now I know in part; then I shall understand fully, Even as I
have been fully understood."*
– I Corinthians 13:12.

I am nearsighted,

   Searching madly,

      Groping for things unseen,

         Dimly proceeding onward,

            I miss the mark.

My perception is limited to that which is near and tangible
   and blind to things in the distance.

Since my perception of distant objects is fuzzy,
   I often deceive myself into thinking that they aren't there
at
    all.

Because of my short-sightedness,
   I doubt the word of those with superior sight.

When they offer me help, I refuse
    and continue to thrash blindly at the unseen world
    around me.

What am I to do, but wait for that day
    when a miracle of love will open my eyes and I will see
    clearly as I am clearly seen?

JUST ONCE

Dwight Parrish

i wish

i could lay with the sun

at our favorite spot

and not get jealous

when she creeps away

in the middle of the nite

to wake up

with someone else.

THE YOOP

Dwight Parrish

hiking

trails

as close to

untamed wilderness

as any barb

could venture

backpack

bearing spirits

egging you closer

to the

unforgiving

edges

of the sand dunes

tranquility

sitting atop

ancient rock formations

peering

down

at the

cool

blue

lake

with its

antagonist

blue-green algae

pondering

miles of multicolored

sandstone cliffs

unplugged

from tall buildings

eyeing

passing motorists and dollar generals’

cliff

diving

from a plateau

thirty feet above

the nearest

watering hole

leaving behind

troubles that

can’t swim

and fears

that are

afraid of heights

absorbing

the melody of

rhythmic waterfalls

cascading

over carved stones

so high up

verse-makers

have to

raise their game

in order to reach

the summit

sleeping

quarters

lost in the forest

a fire pit

surrounded by

plastic chairs

and urban fugitives

sharing information

and "shots"

before

nodding off

under stars

that are wide awake

yep

i long to be a poet in the U.P.

KITTENS

Donna J. Bunner

Kittens, kittens, kittens everywhere,

Kittens near my feet playing and jumping everywhere.

Sounds of pitter patter down the hall the kittens go,

Where their little paws take them, no one in Heaven knows.

Adorable and cute the kittens are for sure.

Fluffiness and furriness bring out the playfulness with

A stir.

Kneading and purring happen often while sitting

On the couch,

Letting us know that the kittens are quite happy

Even after mewing from another kitten's ouch.

Nudges, purrs, and nesting on laps happen often

Along with the sleeping at our feet nightly as the kitty's

Purr silently softens.

Always will know when mealtime is about to happen,

As there is always a Heavenly choir of meows with kittens

Mouth's smacking.

Kittens, kittens, kittens, how can you live without,

Watching the kittens playing will bring joys and smiles

no doubt.

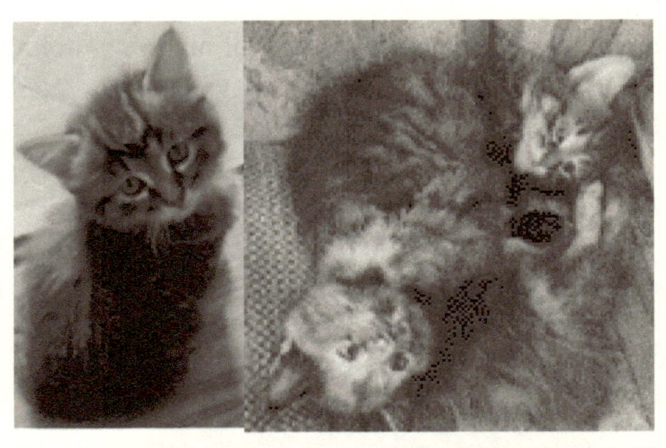

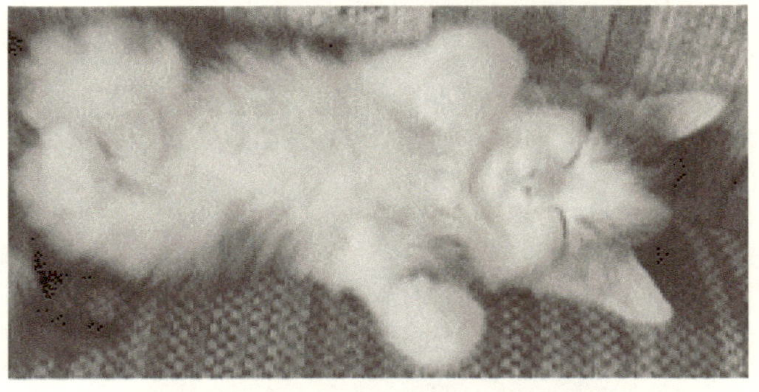

THE VOICE

Donna J. Bunner

The Voice

Did I hear the still small voice?

Was it only in my heart or also in my head?

Did I listen to it and obey?

Did I just ignore it and walk away?

Is it hard to hear?

Did I tune it out?

Did I choose to do my own thing to later be filled with fear and doubt?

Did I forget to do what the voice asked?

Did I complete the requested task?

How can I long to hear the voice?

Definitely in my heart would be the right choice.

WHERE WE COME FROM

My Father's Bookshelf

My Girls (1935)

Man's Place

Benefit of War

Calendar '23

Betrayal

A Crisp Fall Breeze

Change in Quarters

When Life Throws You

Behaviors…

MY FATHER'S BOOKSHELF

Lisa. A Beltz

Its essence dominates the room,

Holding the books most valued by him,

The Holy Bible, Peterson's "Field Guide to the Birds,"
a beaten-up old dictionary

Amongst an eclectic collection that includes

the works of Kipling and Hoyle and Kant,

"The Wisdom of China and India,"

"The Decline and Fall of the Roman Empire,"

Exploits of T. E. Lawrence,

Books of assorted poetry,

An intriguing, well-aged tome in German (which none of
us can read).

To these, decades later, I added

Works of Virgil and Poe and Hayek,

Douglas Adams and Bonhoeffer,

A collection of stories by The Brothers Grimm,

A pocket Constitution,

My dissertation,

A book of Ken-Ken.

(I knew that my mother would never consider "Tuesdays with Morrie.")

He died the day before I became a teen, leaving us happy memories of a man deeply in love with his family.

And books.

And Questions…

Why did <u>those</u> works capture the mind of a man raised in a town too small to be even worthy of that designation, who took college courses in Management in evenings when he was able to snatch blocks of precious moments from an already over-flowing life?

How <u>did</u> the leopard really get his spots?

Do the good die young?

Who decided that Hoyle was an authority on card games?

Why did you leave us so vulnerable?

Why would one kill the albatross?

Did you have to be so good?

Was Nero insane or a frustrated artist, painting out his pain on the canvas of other's lives?

Did you have to die in such a manner, at such a time?

Should only sons beware the Jabberwocky?

Didn't you care that we needed you?

My father's bookshelf holds books and thoughts from a man temporarily beyond my reach.

Reminders of a man who I long to know better. Words sometimes as incomprehensible as "Forgive them, for they know not what they do."

The answers must be in my father's books, but my days and hours are as full as his were.

If only I could separate the chaff from the grain…

If only I had the wisdom to know where to begin…

MY GIRLS (1935)

Harriet Miser, modified by Lisa A. Beltz

Some years ago, I had a bunch of five little girls,

Sometimes their hair was tousled, sometimes, in curls.

Some had eyes that were dark brown and twinkled while passing by,

While other eyes were soft and lustrous and blue as a summer sky.

Each little girl had a very dear place in every act of my life,

Lots of times there was fun and laughter, and sometimes little bits of strife.

Took lots of thinking and planning, my duties I would not shirk,

For it was indeed a great pleasure and not considered hard work.

One day, there came a messenger sent from our God of love,

He plucked one precious flower and took her to live above.

I bowed to God's will, for she went to climb the golden stairs,

This one was just in the middle, leaving two distinct pairs.

Two of them were forced out early to compete with the masses,

While two of them were still at home, just chubby little lasses.

Had to hustle and hurry, both early and late,

While endeavoring to start each day a clean slate.

Years passed rapidly by, and to keep out of a ditch,

And have good clothing for all, took many a stitch.

To make dresses and flounces all trimmed up with lace,

Garments were hanging from every nook in the place.

When night settled down and the day was ended,

Someone had to hold tacks while the shoes were mended.

Oh, we had lots of hard storms, some very bad weather,

But I felt so secure when I had you together.

Treat everyone kindly, for your rights take a stand,

For you have three sisters who will lend you a hand.

As for me, I prefer peace instead of a spat,

But if there must be fighting, I can also do that.

I've expressed my thoughts in these little rhymes,

If you think it worthwhile, just read them sometimes.

As you journey through life, you'll not find another,

Who will cherish and love you any more than your
MOTHER.

Front (left to right): Dora Miser, Harriet Miser, Benjamin Miser, Ruby Clewell Back (left to right): Freddie White, William White, Marcie Lawreance, Frank Lawreance (holding Ruth Lawreance),, Richard Clewell.

Left to right: Ruby, Marcie, Freddie, and Dora Miser.

MAN'S PLACE

Lisa A. Beltz

Man, with all of your great knowledge,

What are you?

Only the rocks live forever.

Rocks, with your great longevity,

What are you?

Not even rocks stand forever.

BENEFIT OF WAR

Dwight Parrish

i think of that camouflage jacket

the lining i came to adore

with spirit and laughter and caring

surviving that jungle of war

the pockets so often were bulging

with joy from the simplest of things

with patience and strength that would clang

fighting wars that each new day would bring

it wrapped me with warmth in the winter

it hid me from brawls in the fall

it brushed off the dirt when i fell

and made sure that i always stood tall

sometimes it would hang in the shadows

but never too far out of view

confronted by enemy lines

springing up just to escort me thru

the heart of that camouflage jacket

is what i so treasure the most

gave meaning and life to the fabric

that made it much more than a coat

the vet who has stood in my foxhole

has been there since i was a child

that jacket he wore oh so proudly

will stay on my mind all the while.

his thrill for baseball feats

his love of o'le reserve

sunday

church was waiting

got dressed and out the door

my mind and thoughts were racing

but god had rest in store

the storm is passing over

i know the rain will end

but today is so much colder

cause this week i lost three friends.

BETRAYAL

Crystal Hoff

As I look back now

I wonder

if our fourteen year friendship

was even worth it now.

Every time I try

to forget

about your betrayal

I just feel like crying.

How

did I not see

the signs

of our friendship

breaking

apart?

Where did things

go wrong?

That you'd turn your back on me

like this.

You knew

I had

trust issues

to begin with

but

you were my friend.

No matter how many times

you apologize

I'll forgive you.

But

once trust is broken

it can't be

repaired.

Trust

needs to be earned

again

but the way you've turned your back on me –

things

will never be

the same between us.

I

get mad

at myself

for not noticing

our friendship

drifting apart

earlier than it did.

I often

question myself

about

what happened to us.

We

used to be

so close

but now

you're just cold

to me.

Letting you go

is the best decision

I've made in my life.

A COOL FALL BREEZE

Crystal Hoff

When it's fall

I can tell

by the

cold

chilly

breeze.

When I feel

the breeze

it brings back

so many unpleasant memories

of feeling

scared

and

alone

wishing

I had

your love

and support.

Even now

I feel like

I'm always

walking on eggshells

around you-

afraid you'll brush

my feelings off

like you did

growing up.

You were

there

then again

you weren't.

You came.

You disappeared.

You touched

my face

gently

then

 again you were gone.

Oh

if you could

only

be like

the gentle breeze

of fall.

CHANGE IN QUARTERS

Dawn E. Dagger

Laundromats were a comfort

When I was young.

They always smelled

Of warm linens

And fresh, floral scents.

A welcome smell,

So different

From the stench of too many

People and animals

Shoved into a too small house.

There was always a space

Just for me

As a young child

In a laundromat.

A corner

With crayons

And blocks

And a little TV

With shows we couldn't get at home.

The laundromats were sometimes empty

Sometimes full

And every stranger

Felt safe

And kind.

Before I realized that my body

Was just meat

For men to stare at

As I tried to wash my clothes.

The laundromats had

Vending machines

With food we normally couldn't afford

In me-sized packaging

For just quarters-

Something we could afford.

And things

I had never seen before-

Like *Frogger*

And lesbians.

The day

My childhood ended

Was the day

That the laundromat felt

Like a threat.

When I realized

I was just

Another spectacle

For the strangers crowded inside.

Where it stank of

Hot mildew

and piss

and everything was sticky.

But, the day

My new life began

Was when I realized

That

Home

Was now the place

Where people were kind,

And things smelled nice,

And we could have food,

And see things

I had never seen before.

WHEN LIFE THROWS YOU

Donna J. Bunner

When life throws you cheese, make a cheeseburger and say, "I'm blessed".

When life throws you a watermelon, spit out the seeds and say, "I'm redeemed".

When life throws you spaghetti, twist the noodles on the fork and say, "I'm forgiven".

When life throws you meatloaf, squirt out the ketchup and say, "I'm healed".

When life throws you a steak, use a steak knife to cut and say, "I'm prosperous".

When life throws you meatballs, add extra sauce and say, "I'm an overcomer".

When life throws you a pickle, open the jar and say, "I'm worthy".

When life throws you corn on the cob, apply the butter and say, "I'm a miracle".

When life throws you Brussel sprouts, add bacon and say, "I'm chosen".

When life throws you chicken nuggets, dip them in barbecue sauce and say, "I'm a conqueror".

When life throws you spinach, steam it and say, "I am strong".

When life throws you cabbage, roll it up and say, "I'm whole".

When life throws you sloppy joes, grab the Manwich and say, "I'm loved".

When life throws you pizza, put on the pepperoni and say, "I'm a believer".

When life throws you nachos, pour out the salsa and say, "I'm a new creation".

When life throws you biscuits, add the gravy and say, "I'm a promise".

When life throws you hot dogs, add the Coney sauce and say, "I'm debt free".

When life throws you marshmallows, roast them over an open fire and say, "I'm a survivor".

And when life seems hard and throws you broccoli, melt the cheese and say, "I'm smiling as at least I'm not throwing tomatoes".

BEHAVIORS...

Donna J. Bunner

Behaviors I place in a box-

along with meltdowns

and added attitudes.

To only come back out and rip the cardboard

wide open to reappear time and time again.

Crying,

arms a-going,

and hand-banging

oh my.

Where is my ripped box to place my cares in?

It would be nice to have masking tape

and a bow to wrap box of

mumbles,

complaining,

and whining

in forever to finally not have a care in the world.

Will it ever be?

No, never.

ABOUT THE AUTHORS

Alexxa Burton

Alexxa has spent most of her life in Ohio when she wasn't busy exploring the planet Miaca. She has recently began dabbling in poetry after a nearly 20 year hiatus.

Her novel, *From Winter*, is her first feature-length novel, and is available on Amazon. When she's not writing, she spends her time in the kitchen creating masterpieces of a different type or spending time with her dogs and cat.

Crystal Hoff

Crystal Hoff has a passion for her family, friends, and faith. She grew up in West Salem Ohio, and graduated from Northwestern High School. She has overcome many challenges in her life, including a turbulent home life, and now writes to inspire others.

Dawn E. Dagger

An avid reader and writer for as long as she can remember, Dawn Dagger is a free-spirited author who loves everything fantastical and caffeinated.

Dawn makes art at every opportunity she can. Whether it's making commentary and gaming YouTube videos, teaching herself the piano, or something entirely new, she's always busy with something.

Her current series include *The Chronicles of Salt and Blood*, and *The Atlantic Island: Mosaics Trilogy*, and the Jonathan Mayberry endorsed novella *DARK*.

Donna J. Bunner

Donna grew up in Norton Ohio. Upon graduation, she received 2 associate degrees, one in Executive Secretary the other in Medical Secretary from the University of Akron. Donna developed a love for the special needs community after attending her daughter's classroom activities in the Multihandicapped classroom. Donna has held several hats during her life from being a single parent to being a medical transcriptionist. She has also served in Special Needs Ministries in Stark County.

Today Donna works as a Direct Support Professional serving the Special Needs Community. Donna enjoys needlepoint with plastic canvas, researching family history, spending time with family, friends, and cats, scrapbooking, Vera Bradley purses, reading Holocaust stories especially The Diary of Anne Frank, and attending church.

Donna is also part of the Massillon Public Library Adult Writing Group as she hopes to create writings about her Faith and Autism.

Dwight Parrish

Dwight Parrish is a retired customer relations supervisor who always had a passion for writing. In the early stages of retirement, he completed a creative writing course at Malone University. He holds a bachelor's degree in finance and a master's degree in business administration.

He enjoys reading, hanging out at the beach, and listening to music. Dwight and his wife Cyndie live in Northeast Ohio. They have (3) children, (7) grandchildren, and (1) great- grandson.

His debut poetry collection, *Sketches of Me*, is an Amazon Bestseller.

Lisa A. Beltz

Lisa developed an intense interest in parasitology while a on month-long field trip in Costa Rica as a student at Malone College (currently Malone University) which led to further studies of immunology and parasitology while a doctoral student in Microbiology and Public Health at Michigan State University.

She began her career in infectious disease research in the Department of Microbiology and Public Health at Michigan State University under the guidance of Dr. Felipe Kierszenbaum with a dissertation entitled "Suppression of Human T Lymphocyte Responses by Trypanosoma cruzi."

MKS Cooper

MKS Cooper began composing poetry at the age of ten. A number of those early, handwritten poems were preserved by her grandmother and mother. Though old, tattered, and somewhat faded, they are some of her favorite treasures.

As an adult, MKS added short stories and novels to her repertoire. Her debut novel, *The Mysteries of Tremont Meadow*, is available through Amazon. She also has a children's illustrated book, *The Christmas Horse*.

MKS lives in Ohio with her husband. They share a large family of children, grandchildren, and great-grandchildren who are scattered around the country in Ohio, Illinois, Florida, Georgia, and California. In her spare time, she enjoys reading, knitting, crocheting, crossword and jigsaw puzzles, and music.